$1-

D1191316

NIKOLA TESLA
AND
THOMAS EDISON

Gareth Stevens
PUBLISHING

Robyn Hardyman

Please visit our website, **www.garethstevens.com**. For a free color catalog of all our high-quality books, call toll free 1-800-542-2595 or fax 1-877-542-2596.

Library of Congress Cataloging-in-Publication Data

Hardyman, Robyn.
Nikola Tesla and Thomas Edison / by Robyn Hardyman.
p. cm. -- (Dynamic duos of science)
Includes index.
ISBN 978-1-4824-1296-3 (pbk.)
ISBN 978-1-4824-1285-7 (6-pack)
ISBN 978-1-4824-1473-8 (library binding)
1. Tesla, Nikola, -- 1856-1943 -- Juvenile literature. 2. Edison, Thomas A. -- (Thomas Alva), -- 1847-1931 -- Juvenile literature. 3. Electrical engineers -- United States -- Biography -- Juvenile literature. 4. Inventors -- United States -- Biography -- Juvenile literature. I. Hardyman, Robyn. II. Title.
TK140.T4 H37 2015
621.3--d23

First Edition

Published in 2015 by
Gareth Stevens Publishing
111 East 14th Street, Suite 349
New York, NY 10003

© Gareth Stevens Publishing

Produced by: Calcium, www.calciumcreative.co.uk
Designed by: Keith Williams
Edited by: Sarah Eason and Jennifer Sanderson
Picture research by: Rachel Blount

Photo credits: Cover: Wikimedia Commons: Library Of Congress/Bachrach (right), Napoleon Sarony (left); Inside: Dreamstime: Americanspirit 40, Czbrat 22, Deymos 39, Geoffrey Kuchera 10, Marie-claire Lander 44, David Larmay 35, Ldambies 31l, Georg Henrik Lehnerer 21, Richie Lomba 15, Adam Radosavljevic 45; Library of Congress: Dickson/William Kennedy-Laurie 42; Shutterstock: Antonio Abrignani 24, Aivolie 32, Anneka 11, Artcphotos 8, Leo Blanchette 37, Chones 1, 18, Bart Everett 29, Zack Frank 33, Frank Peters 5, Ingridat 38, Littleny 4, Stuart Monk 19, Patrick Poendl 41, Chuck Rausin 14, Sakala 28, Stocksnapper 20, Xbrchx 7; Wikimedia Commons: Andrew Balet 13, Euku 43, Flickr/Smithsonian Institution Archives 31r, Matthew Gordon 9, Billy Hathorn 16, Jonathunder 17, Kr. hrv.-slav.-dalm. zemaljska vlada/Kön. kroat.-slav.-dalm. Landes-Regierung 23, LOC/Hunt, Ft. Myers, Fla. published 1914 26, LOC/Look Magazine Collection, Bob Sandberg 25, Ludek 34, Maksim 6, New-York Tribune 36, Zátonyi Sándor 30, Napoleon Sarony 12, Zeljko Filipin 27.

Printed in the United States of America

CPSIA compliance information: Batch #CS15GS: For further information contact Gareth Stevens, New York, New York at 1-800-542-2595.

Contents

CHAPTER 1

Brilliant Scientists

When Thomas Edison (born February 11, 1847) and Nikola Tesla (born July 10, 1856) came into the world, it was very different from today. The railroads were still new, and there were no computers, cars, or telephones. Scientists knew about electricity, but people's homes and city streets were lit only by candles and gas lamps. There were no switches to flip to bring light or power into homes and workplaces.

Edison and Tesla were extraordinary men—two of the greatest pioneers of their time. Edison changed the world in many ways. His scientific experiments resulted in amazing devices that flowed out of the factories that he built next to his laboratories. He was hungry for success and was tireless in his pursuit of it. Often he was improving on the ideas of others, but his vision and determination to push the boundaries of progress were legendary.

Today, we can light up enormous cities, such as Las Vegas, at night thanks to the pioneering work on electricity by Edison.

Many of the inventions that we take for granted today, such as radio, were pioneered by the genius Tesla.

A Man of Ideas

Tesla was a different kind of genius than Edison. He was a man of ideas: more ideas than he could ever test, even in his long life. He was often more interested in developing these ideas than in creating practical inventions that used them. Nevertheless, he did put some of them into practice. Like Edison, he worked hard to bring electricity to the world in ways that would change it forever.

IN THEIR OWN WORDS

Edison said:

"Opportunity is missed by most people because it is dressed in overalls and looks like work."

Early Beginnings

Both Edison and Tesla had a passion for finding out how things work. Their backgrounds were ordinary, but even from a young age, they both showed great scientific potential.

Edison as a Child

Thomas Alva Edison was born in 1847 in Ohio. When he was seven, his family moved to Port Huron, Michigan. Edison was often sick as a young child, so he could not go to school until he was eight. However, that did not stop him being inquisitive. His endless questions annoyed his teachers, so his mother took him out of school and taught him herself. She also let him do his own chemical experiments in a laboratory he set up in the cellar. After a childhood illness, Edison became almost completely deaf. Despite this, he went on to become one of the world's greatest inventors.

As a boy, Edison was always asking questions and eager to learn more about the world.

BEHIND THE SCIENCE

Edison looked for new business ventures from a young age. The railroads were still new in the 1800s, and Edison loved them. At the age of 12, he started riding the trains and even conducted chemical experiments on board! Edison also sold newspapers, drinks, and vegetables from his garden to passengers.

Tesla's birthplace in Smiljan Lika, Croatia, is today a memorial center to the outstanding scientist.

Tesla as a Child

Nikola Tesla was born in 1856 in Smiljan, in the part of former Austria-Hungary that is now Croatia. The idea of inventing things may have come from Tesla's mother, who was forever inventing small appliances at home in her spare time. Tesla was an excellent student at school, where his passion was science. He eventually moved away to study at a university in Prague in Czechoslovakia, which is now in the Czech Republic.

Trains and the Telegraph

Edison's early experiences on the trains set him up for his career. He was longing to put his energy into something really useful, and one day the chance to do so came along.

It was an act of bravery that gave Edison his first break. One day at the railroad station, when he was just 15, he rescued the young son of the stationmaster from being hit by a loose wagon that was rolling down the track.

The stationmaster asked Edison what he would like as a reward for saving the boy's life. He replied that he wanted to learn how to work the telegraph machine. Edison's wish was granted.

Edison worked long hours at the depot at Port Huron, Michigan.

Edison's First Invention

Edison worked as a telegraph operator for six years, traveling around the United States. All the while, he was thinking up ways to make the telegraph system work better. At 16, he made his first invention, called an automatic repeater. It sent telegraph messages between unmanned stations. The messages could then be translated when the operator arrived. The pressure of "live" translation was a thing of the past.

BEHIND THE SCIENCE

In the 1800s, the telegraph was the fastest way to send a message over a long distance. An operator tapped out the message in Morse code, an "alphabet" of dots and dashes, at one end of a long wire. The message was received miles away at the other end of the wire. The United States was soon covered with telegraph wires.

This statue of the young Edison stands in memory of him at the depot at Port Huron, Michigan.

Setting Up

Edison enjoyed his work, but he longed to branch out and develop more of his ideas for inventions. He could see a world of opportunity just waiting to be grasped.

In 1868, Edison's long work on the telegraph paid off. When he showed the Western Union Telegraph Company in Boston how it could be improved, they paid him a reward of $40,000. This meant that he could pursue his dream of bringing his other inventions to life. He set up a workshop in Newark, New Jersey, in 1869 and for five years worked hard. His first ever patent was for an electric vote-counter to use in elections. This made counting votes much faster, but at the time, nobody wanted to buy it. From then on, Edison decided to invent only things that people really wanted.

Telegraph offices were often found at railroad stations in the 1800s.

Edison worked for years on the Morse code telegraph transmitter.

Becoming a Boss

Edison hired engineers to develop his plans so that he could sell them. Many of these men, or "muckers" as they were called, were loyal to their boss and stayed with him throughout his career. Edison found personal happiness at this time, too. In 1871, when he was 24 years old, he married Mary Stillwell. They had three children, but family life was no match for Edison's endless wish to work.

BEHIND THE SCIENCE

A patent is the official right given to an inventor to make or sell his or her invention. It also prevents other people from copying the invention. Patents protect the invention only for a limited number of years.

11

CHAPTER 2

Career Building

Edison's career was well underway while over in Europe, Tesla was finishing his education and getting ready to follow his own career path.

Tesla had at first intended to specialize in physics and math, but he soon found that he was fascinated with electricity. Just like Edison, he had worked first on the telegraph system, in his case in Austria. In 1881, he became an electrical engineer with a telephone company in Budapest, Hungary. It was there that he had one of his brilliant ideas. Walking with a friend in the city park, he came up with the new idea of a rotating magnetic field. He drew a diagram of it in the sand with a stick. This basic principle of physics was a key part of Tesla's later invention of a new kind of electric motor—the induction motor.

IN THEIR OWN WORDS

Tesla said of his desire to understand the scientific principles in the world around us:

"The desire that guides me in all I do is the desire to harness the forces of nature to the service of mankind."

Tesla was always motivated by the desire to discover new things that could be used to help people and to make their lives better.

Menlo Park

Edison continued to work on the telegraph in Newark. In 1876, he built a large new laboratory at Menlo Park, New Jersey, and called it his "Invention Factory." It was the first industrial research laboratory in the world. Edison and his helpers were going to develop inventions that would change people's lives—and make Edison famous.

Edison's laboratory at Menlo Park included an organ on the back wall, so he and his workers could have music during mealtimes.

Carbon Transmitter

Edison worked his men hard. He expected a lot from them, but everyone was excited about the possibilities in their work. Edison promised to produce "a minor invention every ten days and a big thing every six months or so."

The latest invention, the telephone, became the focus of Edison's efforts. In 1876, Alexander Graham Bell had patented the telephone. With this amazing machine, people could talk to each other over distances for the very first time. The telegraph began to look old-fashioned. There was a problem with the new technology, however. Voices on the telephone sounded very faint and carried only for a few miles. Edison carried out thousands of experiments to improve the system. Eventually, he figured it out.

Carbon transmitters were widely used in telephones in the United States right up to the 1980s. This is an early model.

BEHIND THE SCIENCE

The first telephone call was made on March 10, 1876. Alexander Graham Bell spoke into the mouthpiece: "Mr. Watson—Come here—I want to see you." Mr. Watson, who was listening at the receiving end in an adjoining room, heard the words clearly.

The Age of the Telephone

Edison invented a small component called a carbon transmitter. This was the microphone in the telephone's handset that transmitted the sound of the voice. At last, people could hear each other clearly. Western Union paid Edison $100,000 for his invention. The age of the telephone had begun.

The Phonograph

In 1877, Edison invented an entirely new kind of machine. This was the first machine that could record sound and then play it back. He called it the phonograph, and it made "the Wizard of Menlo Park" famous around the world.

The phonograph allowed people to listen to recorded music for the very first time.

Before the invention of the phonograph, people could enjoy music only if it were played live. Edison's idea was to record it using a needle that would press grooves corresponding to sound waves into a rotating cylinder coated with tin. The recording could then be played back on the phonograph, using another needle to trace the grooves. Edison got his mechanic, John Kruesi, to build the machine. Edison spoke into a cylinder wrapped in tin, saying: "Mary had a little lamb." The phonograph played his words back to him!

A standard cylinder played about two minutes of music or other sounds. They were later replaced by flat records, which played for a longer time.

Edison's Favorite Invention

The tin-coated cylinders could be played just a few times before they wore out. Over the next few years, Edison developed longer-lasting ones made of a hard wax. He loved the phonograph and called it his favorite invention. Over time, his cylinder players were replaced with ones that played flat records, but the basic mechanism always remained the same.

IN THEIR OWN WORDS

Edison said of the phonograph:

"This is my baby and I expect it to grow up and be a big feller and support me in my old age."

Let There Be Light!

When you walk into a dark room and flip a switch, think of Edison! He and his team worked tirelessly to invent an electric lightbulb that would last.

In the mid-1800s, several scientists realized that a thread inside a glass bulb could be made to light up by passing a small amount of electricity through it. They experimented with creating lightbulbs, but the light glowed only for a few moments and the bulbs kept exploding. In 1878, Edison was determined to solve the problem.

BEHIND THE SCIENCE

Inside an electric lightbulb, there is no air. The air is removed with a pump to create a vacuum. Without air, the filament cannot burn up. It simply glows.

Edison's patent for his new invention was issued in January 1880.

Edison's first successful lightbulb marked a turning point for the world. It paved the way for scenes such as this one that we see every day on Broadway in New York City.

Lighting Up the United States

Edison experimented with thousands of different materials for the thread inside the bulb, called a filament. These included hair and coconut fiber. Finally, in 1879, he tried a cotton thread that had been carbonized, or burned, to make it hard. The months of hard work paid off. The filament glowed brightly for at least 13 hours. Edison did not stop there. He wanted to improve his lightbulb. He soon found that carbonized bamboo fibers worked even better than cotton. This was very exciting! Edison lit the whole of Menlo Park with his new bulbs. That was just the beginning—his plan was to light up all of New York City.

Power to the People

Edison knew there was little point in inventing lightbulbs that worked if the electricity that powered them could not reach the streets and people's homes. He wanted everyone to benefit from his inventions.

In 1881, Edison formed the Edison Electric Light Company in New York City. Its function was to generate electricity and distribute it around the city. At that time, gas lamps lit the streets but that was about to change. Edison helped to build the first commercial electric power plant in the United States on Pearl Street in Manhattan. The power was generated by huge steam engines.

BEHIND THE SCIENCE

When customers are using electricity, the power company must know how much they have used, so that they can bill them for it. Edison invented a meter called a Webermeter to be installed in customers' homes to measure their usage.

Although Pearl Street Station burned down in 1890, Edison was determined to bring electricity to New York City.

At night Earth seen from space is a blaze of lights. This lighting of our modern world all began with the work of Edison and his team.

A Huge Success

On the afternoon of September 4, 1882, Edison stood proudly in the Pearl Street power plant. It was the moment of truth and the point at which everyone would see the magnitude of his work. A total of eighty-five customers had paid to be the first to receive electricity in their homes. Their houses had been wired up and fitted with 400 lightbulbs. As the chief electrician pulled the switch, the lights went on in 85 different places at once! It was a great success, and by 1884 Pearl Street was serving 508 customers with more than 10,000 lamps. Edison knew this was a huge opportunity not only to change the world but to also make a lot of money. The inventor realized that soon everyone would want to buy the electrical components that his company made.

CHAPTER 3

Working Together

Both Edison and Tesla were interested in how best to distribute electricity. At first the two men got along well, but when they clashed over their work, the sparks certainly began to fly.

In 1882, Tesla started working for the Continental Edison Company in France. He worked on installing lighting systems based on Edison's inventions. His childhood dream had been to go to the United States, and in 1884, at the age of 28, he moved to New York City. On the journey, he was robbed of his ticket and his luggage, and he arrived in New York City with almost nothing. However, he did have a letter of recommendation for Edison from a man called Charles Batchelor. Batchelor's letter said: "I know two great men. One is you and the other is this young man."

The huge power plants we have today originated with the work of Edison and Tesla on producing and distributing electricity for lots of people.

This is Tesla's passport from 1883. He moved to the United States in 1884 and remained there for the rest of his life.

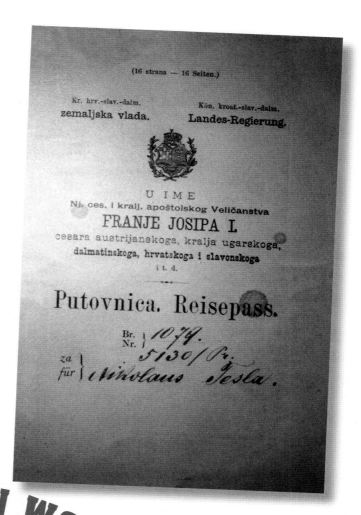

The Brilliance of Tesla

Tesla was soon working directly for Edison at the Edison Machine Works. Edison could see that his new recruit was very bright and able, and realized the potential riches that Tesla could bring to his business. Tesla quickly progressed to working on some of the company's most difficult projects.

IN THEIR OWN WORDS

Tesla was very proud to be a US citizen. In 1919, he said:

"...the papers, which 30 years ago conferred upon me the honor of American citizenship, are always kept in a safe, while my orders, diplomas, degrees, gold medals, and other distinctions are packed away in old trunks."

Generators

Electricity is a form of energy. It can be made by burning fuels such as coal and natural gas. In Edison's power plants, burning fuels produced steam that powered steam engines. The movement in the steam engines was converted into electrical energy by another machine called a generator. Generators provided all the power for the electricity supply that served streets, homes, and businesses.

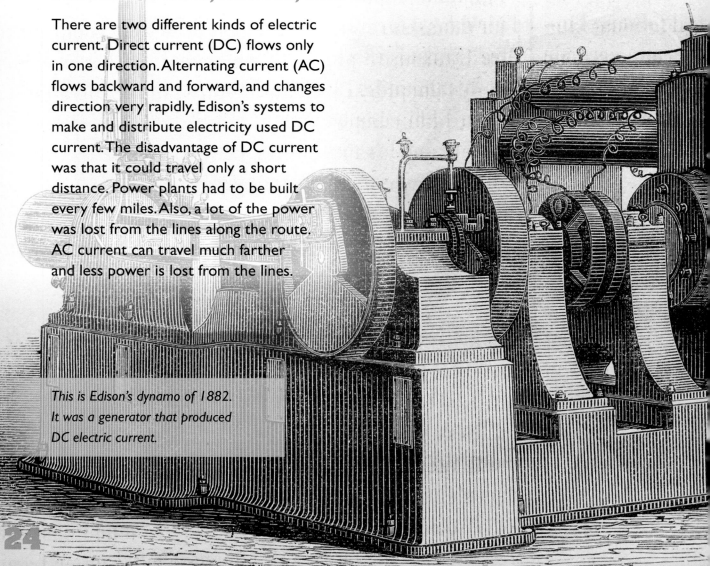

There are two different kinds of electric current. Direct current (DC) flows only in one direction. Alternating current (AC) flows backward and forward, and changes direction very rapidly. Edison's systems to make and distribute electricity used DC current. The disadvantage of DC current was that it could travel only a short distance. Power plants had to be built every few miles. Also, a lot of the power was lost from the lines along the route. AC current can travel much farther and less power is lost from the lines.

This is Edison's dynamo of 1882. It was a generator that produced DC electric current.

Tensions at Work

Edison's systems used generators called dynamos, which produced the DC current. They were not very efficient, and it was this problem that led to arguments between Edison and Tesla.

The Brooklyn Dodgers baseball team and their fans understood the dangers of exposed electric wires!

BEHIND THE SCIENCE

The Brooklyn Dodgers baseball team got their name because residents had to "dodge" shocks from electric trolley tracks.

End of the Partnership

Edison and Tesla were very different personalities. Perhaps it was inevitable that this and their ambitions would lead to them no longer working together.

Edison knew that AC current worked better over long distances. He did not think, however, that it could be used in power systems because of its higher voltage, or strength. He put Tesla to work on the problem of redesigning his existing dynamos so that the DC system could work better. In 1885, Tesla claimed he could make huge improvements to the system. He said that Edison then made the following promise to him: "There's $50,000 in it for you—if you can do it."

Edison (left), John Burroughs (center), and Henry Ford (right) are today considered the fathers of modern business.

This statue in Zagreb commemorates Tesla and his contribution to science in his home country, Croatia.

IN THEIR OWN WORDS

Edison never stopped testing his thousands of ideas to see if they worked. He said:

"Many of life's failures are people who did not realize how close they were to success when they gave up."

Tesla Resigns

After months of work, Tesla did as he had promised and solved the problem. Edison refused to pay up, claiming he had been joking. "You don't understand our American humor," he told Tesla. He offered Tesla a small raise in salary instead. Furious, Tesla refused and resigned from his job. From then on, he was going to develop his ideas on his own. The paths of these two geniuses would never cross again.

27

CHAPTER 4

Tesla Works Alone

Tesla had left the protection of Edison's company. If he was going to develop his ideas, he needed financial backing. Luckily for him, he found it from two men, Charles Peck and Alfred S. Brown. They helped him set up a laboratory just a few blocks away from Edison's and encouraged him to get to work.

Tesla's great breakthrough was to invent an AC motor. This used his earlier idea of the rotating magnetic field. He soon invented and patented AC generators, too. By 1887, he had patented a complete AC electrical system, including generators, transmission lines, and lighting. When Tesla gave a lecture on it to the American Institute of Electrical Engineers, it caused a sensation. This new system seemed to be so much better than Edison's.

At the World's Fair in Chicago in 1893, Tesla demonstrated the principles of the rotating magnetic field and the induction motor with this device, called Tesla's egg. The egg stood upright and spun around.

Edison's DC system is still used in the electrical systems of cars and some trains.

Powering the World

Edison did not agree. A "War of Currents" began between the two men. Tesla met an engineer and businessman called George Westinghouse, who was determined to bring the AC system to the whole nation. He paid Tesla for his patents and supported his work. Edison was furious and launched a campaign against them, but in the end, the superiority of the AC system was no match for him. When Tesla's system was chosen to illuminate 100,000 lamps at the prestigious World's Fair in Chicago in 1893, the winner was clear. Tesla's AC system became the standard power system all over the world. It remains so today.

BEHIND THE SCIENCE

Edison's direct current may have lost the battle in power supply, but it did not disappear completely.

Sparks and Lights

The Tesla coil is a truly showy invention. Many thought that this was remarkable coming from a man who was not at all showy himself. In fact, Tesla liked to work alone, testing his ideas for a long time in his head before he ever started to make things.

Tesla patented the Tesla coil in 1891. This device uses AC to create very high voltages of electricity. This makes dramatic sparks and sheets of electric flame, a little like creating lightning on demand! Tesla demonstrated his 1890 invention in his laboratory in New York City to an astonished audience. Tesla coils are still used for entertainment today.

This huge original Tesla coil is now in the Nikola Tesla Memorial Center in Croatia.

We take neon lights for granted today, but in the late 1800s they were revolutionary.

The 1893 Chicago World's Fair was held to celebrate the 400th anniversary of Christopher Columbus's arrival in the New World in 1492. More than 27 million people attended it during its six-month run.

A New Kind of Light

Tesla tried out many new ideas. One of these was a new kind of electric lightbulb. Edison's lightbulbs were incandescent, meaning they gave off light from a burning filament inside. A lot of the energy was lost as heat. Tesla developed some of the first neon lights, which he showed at the 1893 Chicago World's Fair. He also developed early fluorescent lights. Both of these used gas inside the bulb instead of a filament, and the gas used energy more efficiently.

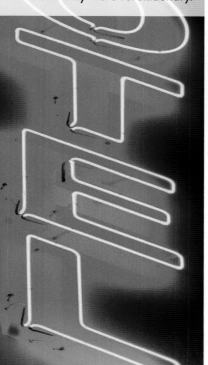

BEHIND THE SCIENCE

Fluorescence is when a substance which has absorbed light from another source gives off that light slowly over time. It occurs in nature and had been known for several hundred years, but Tesla was a pioneer in developing its use in lighting.

31

Hydroelectric Power

As a boy in Croatia, Tesla had seen pictures of Niagara Falls. He remembered how they had made him feel. "Someday I'll harness that power," he had said. The time had come to make his childhood dream come true.

Niagara Falls is a collection of three huge waterfalls on the border between the United States and Canada. Immense volumes of water from the Niagara River crash down more than 160 feet (50 m). This generates a massive amount of power. Scientists had been working for some time on ways to harness this power to create electricity.

The energy in the falling water of waterfalls such as Niagara Falls is used to make electricity in hydroelectric power plants.

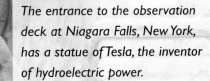

The entrance to the observation deck at Niagara Falls, New York, has a statue of Tesla, the inventor of hydroelectric power.

Super Power Plant

Westinghouse won the contract to develop the project, and in 1895 Tesla designed the world's first large-scale hydroelectric plant. It had two huge generators that used Tesla's new AC techniques, making them even more efficient than his previous systems. On opening day, electricity flowed without a hitch. The plant was so successful that some of its output was transmitted 22 miles (35.4 km) away to Buffalo, New York. This would have been completely impossible with a DC system. It opened up a new world of possibility: electric power could now be taken to every home in the United States. At last, Tesla was famous.

IN THEIR OWN WORDS

In his speech at the opening ceremony for the plant, Tesla said of the project:

"It is a monument worthy of our scientific age, a true monument of enlightenment and of peace. It signifies the subjugation of natural forces to the service of man, the discontinuance of barbarous methods, the relieving of millions from want and suffering."

Tesla the Pioneer

Within a few years, the power plant at Niagara Falls was supplying New York City about 400 miles (644 km) away. Now Tesla had his sights set on new worlds of experimentation. During his long career, he registered more than 111 patents in the United States and about 300 worldwide.

A big new area of work for Tesla was radio. He was looking at ways of sending energy wirelessly from one place to another. Radio resulted from the work of many people, but it was Tesla who worked out the basic technology that made it possible. He registered the first radio patents, and in 1893 he gave a lecture explaining how it worked. This was two years before Marconi began work on radio. Marconi later claimed to be its inventor and won a Nobel Prize for it. It was not until 1943 that Marconi's radio patents were shown to be invalid, and Tesla was finally accepted as radio's true inventor. He had died a few months before.

A radio company in Prague named itself Tesla after radio's inventor, and created this magnificent window in the city.

TESLA
Radio

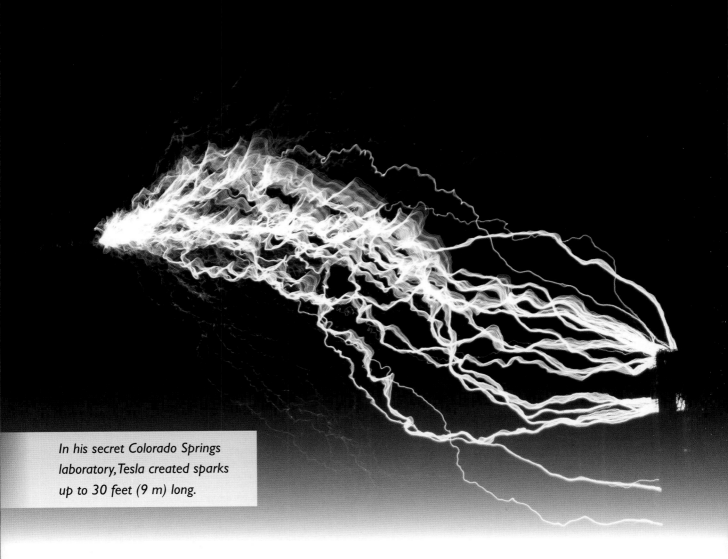

In his secret Colorado Springs laboratory, Tesla created sparks up to 30 feet (9 m) long.

IN THEIR OWN WORDS

When he was told that Marconi was sending wireless radio messages across the Atlantic Ocean, Tesla replied:

"Marconi is a good fellow. Let him continue. He is using 17 of my patents."

Spectacular Electricity

In 1899, Tesla built a secret laboratory in Colorado Springs, Colorado. There he did spectacular experiments with high voltage electricity, shooting huge sparks and flashes across the room.

Wardenclyffe Tower

In the early 1900s, Tesla was living in the Waldorf Astoria Hotel in New York City and working on more ideas than ever. Although he lived and worked alone, he wanted to show people his inventions. He invited famous people and the press to grand dinners in the hotel and then took a select few to his laboratory to see his amazing work for themselves.

One of his most important supporters was the US banker John Pierpont "J. P." Morgan. With his financial help, from 1901 to 1905, Tesla developed his boldest project yet. This was the Wardenclyffe Tower and laboratory in Shoreham, Long Island. It was an amazingly ambitious idea and so far ahead of its time: to build a communications system that would cover the whole world. The Tower would generate electricity that could be transmitted by rods sunk hundreds of feet into the ground, right through the center of Earth. This electricity could then be taken and used freely by everyone, everywhere. Tesla loved this idea of progress being available to all.

This article in the New York Tribune *in August 1901 announced Tesla's plans for his wireless telegraphy project.*

TESLA READY FOR BUSINESS.

HE HAS BOUGHT THE LAND FOR HIS WIRELESS TELEGRAPHY STATION AND LET THE CONTRACTS FOR THE BUILDINGS.

Nikola Tesla's plans for a transatlantic wireless telegraphic system are now so well in hand that he has bought a site for the station on the Long Island shore, and has agents looking for a suitable place for a station on the British coast. The station in this country will be at Wardenclyffe, on the Sound, nine miles east of Port Jefferson. Mr. Tesla has purchased two hundred acres of land in that vicinity, and closed contracts yesterday for the necessary buildings.

Five or six buildings will be erected on different parts of the tract, the largest of which is to be one hundred feet square and several stories high. It will contain, Mr. Tesla says, one of the most complete electrical plants that can be purchased. Three hundred and fifty horsepower will be developed, and the total cost will be nearly $150,000. The other buildings will be used for the electrical experiments with which Mr. Tesla is now engaged, including a system of lighting by diffused light. He will probably give up his present laboratory, at No. 46 East Houston-st., and make his headquarters at Wardenclyffe.

Mr. Tesla has been working for several years with his system of wireless telegraphy, and believes that he has advanced far enough to warrant a change from the experimental to the commercial stage. He says it will not be long before he will be transmitting commercial messages between Wardenclyffe and Europe without the use of wires or cables.

When seen at the Waldorf-Astoria Hotel last night Mr. Tesla said:

"I would have been sending messages across the ocean without the use of wires by this time if the public were not so hard to convince that it could be done. It takes time to assure people of the truth of new discoveries. It was six or eight years before people believed in my system of transmitting electric power. Now it is used everywhere. I cannot tell you just how far I have advanced in the perfection of my system of telegraphy but soon to be able to sh—

36

Failure of Tesla's Dream

J. P. Morgan, however, was not so keen. If the electricity was free, how could anyone make money from the scheme? He withdrew his financial support from Wardenclyffe and the project collapsed.

This huge landmark was 187 feet (57 m) high, capped by a 68-foot (20 m) copper dome. In 2012, campaigners succeeded in saving Tesla's old laboratory at Wardenclyffe from demolition. It will be converted into a museum and science center as a tribute to the scientist's life and work.

IN THEIR OWN WORDS

Tesla imagined the rods at the Wardenclyffe Tower would:

"... get a grip of the Earth ... so that the whole of this globe can quiver."

A Sad End

Tesla was devastated by the failure of his Wardenclyffe project. He carried on working, but in the end, his fame declined and his money ran out. In sharp contrast to Edison's fame and fortune, Tesla eventually died alone and in poverty.

Tesla worked on new ideas, including X-rays, radar, and robotics. He would invite the press to parties on his birthday to announce his new inventions, and the articles they published were popular with the public. He gave groundbreaking lectures to other scientists and inspired young people to take up careers in electrical science.

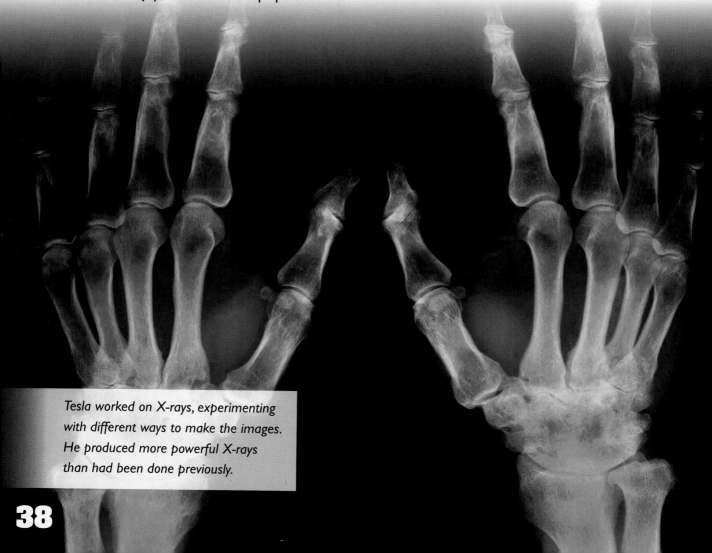

Tesla worked on X-rays, experimenting with different ways to make the images. He produced more powerful X-rays than had been done previously.

This monument to Tesla was unveiled at Niagara Falls in 2006. He stands on an AC motor, one of the 700 inventions he patented.

Dying in Poverty

In 1917, Tesla was awarded the Edison medal, the most prestigious prize in the United States for electrical engineering. In his speech presenting Tesla with the medal, Vice President Behrend of the Institute of Electrical Engineers said: "Were we to seize and eliminate from our industrial world the result of Mr. Tesla's work, the wheels of industry would cease to turn, our electric cars and trains would stop, our towns would be dark, and our mills would be idle and dead. His name marks an epoch in the advance of electrical science." Tesla spent all his money on experiments, and on January 7, 1943, one of the world's greatest scientists died in room 3327 of the New Yorker Hotel.

BEHIND THE SCIENCE

On his seventy-fifth birthday in 1931, Tesla appeared on the cover of *Time* magazine. He received letters of congratulations from more than 70 leading scientists, which were bound into a book and presented to him.

Later Innovations

Thomas Edison, meanwhile, was also working as hard as ever on a range of projects. Some were a huge success, while others ended in failure. However, for Edison, that was all part of the road to progress.

In 1886, Edison remarried, and with his wife and children, he lived in a house called Glenmont in West Orange, New Jersey. This was right by his laboratory and the factories that made the things he invented. In the 1890s, he was determined to find a way to extract iron ore from rock using powerful magnets. He poured millions of dollars into the project and almost went bankrupt. Finally, he had to admit defeat and abandon the venture.

Edison bought Glenmont in 1886 as a wedding gift for his second wife, Mina.

Edison was way ahead of his time in his work on developing a battery for electric cars.

A Vision for the Future

Another of Edison's ideas was more successful. He loved cars, which were newly invented, and he believed that one day they would run on electricity. He began working on a battery that could store enough electricity to run a car for 100 miles (160.9 km) without recharging. We know today that he was definitely onto something. At the time, however, gasoline was so cheap and plentiful that there was little need for his electric-powered car.

BEHIND THE SCIENCE

Edison's work on batteries became his most profitable invention. They were used in miner's headlamps and railroad signals, and his friend Henry Ford used them in his Model T cars. His work also formed the basis of today's work on electric cars.

Working to the End

Edison was always looking for ways to put electricity to use to transform people's lives. This could be at work or at home, for comfort or for pleasure. One of his later inventions has shaped the world of entertainment ever since.

Edison invented a machine called a kinetoscope. This was a viewing machine used by one person at a time to see a short film of moving images. A series of images of a piece of action was taken on film. The film was then passed through the kinetoscope so that the images seemed to "join up" and the subject seemed to move. This technique was the basis of all film projection for decades to come. The first ever commercial exhibition of motion pictures took place in New York City on April 14, 1894, using 10 kinetoscopes in a "peephole parlor."

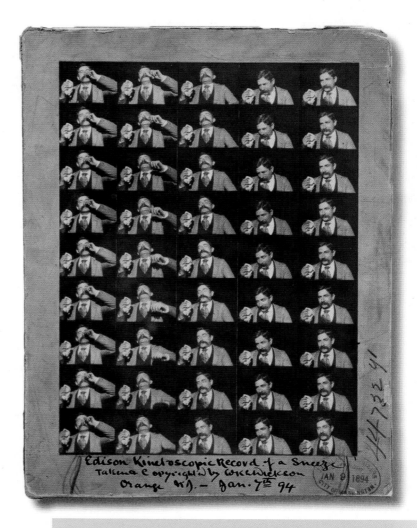

This is the series of images used to make Fred Ott's Sneeze, *the first identifiable motion picture, in 1894. It was shot by Edison's employee, William K. L. Dickson.*

The Edison Botanic Research Laboratory was built by Edison, his friend Henry Ford, and Harvey Firestone to conduct research into rubber. It was built in 1928 and was the headquarters for Edison and his staff. It closed in 1936, after Edison's death.

Edison's Last Project

Another of Edison's more ambitious schemes was to replace the United States' poor quality homes with concrete houses. Concrete from Edison's Portland Cement company were poured into giant, house-shaped molds in one go, creating a cheap, strong house. He even proposed furnishing them with poured concrete furniture! The houses never caught on, so Edison turned his attention to looking for a new way to make rubber instead. He worked on this last project until his death on October 18, 1931, at the age of 84.

IN THEIR OWN WORDS

Edison said:

"Genius is 1 percent inspiration and 99 percent perspiration."

Dynamic Differences

For much of the twentieth century, history assumed all inventions in electricity and lighting came from one man, Thomas Edison. His work was remarkable, but in fact it was Nikola Tesla who pioneered the electrical system that is in standard use around the world today—the AC system.

It is always the case in science that individuals expand on the work of others who came before them. Both Edison and Tesla did this. Edison was more capable of commercializing his inventions. He put his men to work to turn his ideas into products that would sell well and make him very rich. Tesla was much less able to commercialize his work. He always thought through an idea in his head for a very long time before he began experimenting with models. He let others take his brilliant ideas and make them commercially successful for themselves.

This statue of Edison stands in the grounds of his estate at Fort Myers, Florida. Today, the estate is open to the public as a museum all about the life and work of this energetic pioneer and businessman.

$$T = \frac{Wb}{m^2}$$

Tesla has a unit of measurement named after him, as shown on the markings on this banknote. A "tesla" is a unit of the strength of a magnetic field.

Pioneering Scientists

Tesla's pioneering contribution to electricity was only part of his life's work. His other inventions and technologies have made much of today's technology possible. Tesla was looking way ahead of his contemporaries to the future. Edison found fame and riches in his own lifetime. He too explored new technologies and made appliances that changed science and people's lives forever.

IN THEIR OWN WORDS

Tesla said:

"Let the future tell the truth and evaluate each one according to his work and accomplishments. The present is theirs; the future, for which I really worked, is mine."

Glossary

alternating current (AC) an electric current that flows backward and forward and changes direction very rapidly

bankrupt when a person has no money and cannot pay their debts

carbon transmitter a microphone in the handset of a telephone that transmitted the sound of the voice

direct current (DC) an electric current that flows in one direction only

dynamos electric motors that work with DC current

filament the thread inside a lightbulb that glows to give off light

fluorescent light a lightbulb using gas rather than a filament to give off light

generators machines that produce electricity from another kind of energy

hydroelectric power using the energy in moving water to generate electricity

incandescent describing a lightbulb that gives off light from a burning filament inside

kinetoscope a machine for one person to watch short films

magnetic field the space in which a magnetic force can be detected; a magnetic field is created when electricity is passed through a piece of metal

Morse code an alphabet of dots and dashes used for sending messages along a wire

motor a device that uses electricity to make an appliance work

neon light a lightbulb that gives off light using gas inside it rather than a filament

Nobel Prize a very prestigious international prize awarded every year for an outstanding achievement in an area of science or culture

patent a legal right for an inventor to make or sell an invention for a fixed period of time

phonograph a machine that can play back recorded sounds

telegraph a system for sending messages over long distances using wires and Morse code

Tesla coil a device that uses AC to create very high voltages of electricity

vacuum a space where all the matter has been removed

voltage the strength of an electric current

For More Information

Books

Electricity and Magnetism (Usborne Understanding Science). Monterey, CA: National Geographic Learning, 2010.

Jenner, Caryn. *Thomas Edison: The Great Inventor* (DK Readers). New York, NY: DK Children, 2007.

Parker, Steve. *Electricity* (DK Eyewitness Books). New York, NY: DK Children, 2013.

Rusch, Elizabeth. *How Nikola Tesla Lit Up the World* (Electrical Wizard). Somerville, Mass: Candlewick Press, 2013.

Websites

Find out about Tesla's most famous inventions at:
science.howstuffworks.com/innovation/famous-inventors/famous-nikola-tesla-inventions.htm

There are some unusual bits of information about Tesla at:
www.pbs.org/newshour/rundown/2013/07/5-things-you-didnt-know-about-nikola-tesla.html

This is a great site about Edison:
invention.smithsonian.org/centerpieces/edison

Index